For Alice, David and Helen.
Love C.F.

Oxford University Press, Great Clarendon Street, Oxford OX2 6DP

Oxford New York

Athens Auckland Bangkok Bogotá Buenos Aires
Calcutta Cape Town Chennai Dar es Salaam
Delhi Florence Hong Kong Istanbul Karachi
Kuala Lumpur Madrid Melbourne Mexico City
Mumbai Nairobi Paris São Paulo Singapore
Taipei Tokyo Toronto Warsaw

and associated companies in
Berlin Ibadan

Oxford is a trade mark of Oxford University Press

Text Copyright © Richard Edwards 1997
Illustrations Copyright © Chris Fisher 1997

A CIP catalogue record for this book is available from the British Library

ISBN 0-19-910-453-0 (hardback)
ISBN 0-19-910-478-6 (paperback)
3 5 7 9 10 8 6 4

Printed in China

Nonsense
Nursery
Rhymes

Poems by Richard Edwards
Illustrated by Chris Fisher

OXFORD UNIVERSITY PRESS

A a

Andy Dandy's legs were bandy,
Andy's legs were bent,
Through Andy Dandy's bandy legs
The trains to Scotland went.

Bb

Bobby Shafto's gone to sea,
Sailing with a chimpanzee,
They'll be back at half past three,
Bonnie Bobby Shafto.

C c

Cock a doodle doo!
I think I've caught the flu,
Shiver, shiver, cough, cough,
Atchoo! Atchoo! Atchoo!

Dd

D octor Foster went to Gloucester

On a winter's day.

An icicle froze

On the end of his nose

And didn't fall off till May.

E e

Elsie Marley looks so fine,
Dancing down the washing line.
Will you be my valentine,
Lovely Elsie Marley?

Ff

Fee fi fo fum
Little Freddie's looking glum.
How to make him giggle?
Give his toe a wiggle.

Gg

Georgie Porgie, pudding and pie,
Thought he'd catch a fish to fry,
Cast a line above his head,
Caught an aeroplane instead.

H h

Humpty Dumpty sat on a wall,
Humpty Dumpty had a great fall.
He didn't get bruised, he didn't get bumped,
Humpty Dumpty bungee-jumped.

Ii

I had a little nut tree,
I gave the tree a whack,
The tree said "Oi!
You naughty boy!"
And whacked me sharply back.

J j

Jack Sprat could eat no fat,
No sausages, no stew,
His beard was much too bristly
And it wouldn't let things through.

K k

Katie Beardie had a cow
That learnt to drive. Don't ask me how.
The other cows just moo or sleep,
But Katie's cow goes Beep! Beep! Beep!

L l

Little Bo Peep has washed her sheep,
They'd got so grey and greasy,
But after a scrub
In a soapy tub
They came out white and fleecy.

M m

Mary, Mary, quite contrary,
What does your garden hide?
Beetles and bugs,
Slithery slugs
And shells with snails inside.

Nn

Nellie Bligh
Caught a fly
And kept it as a pet,
Taking it to school with her
To learn the alphabet.

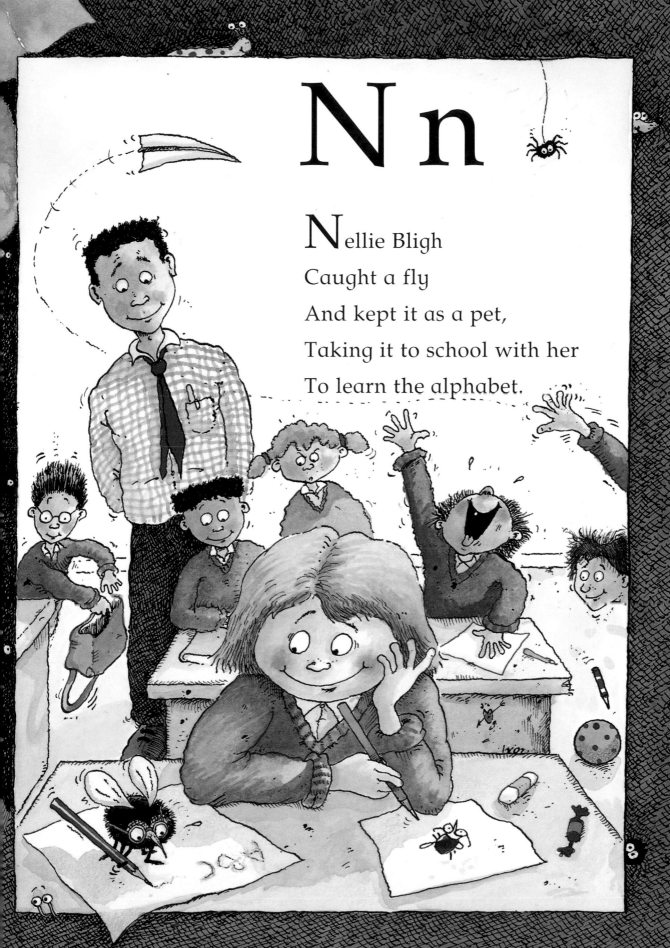

Oo

Old King Cole was a merry old soul,
His crown was tall and twisty.
It had a flashing light on top
For when the nights were misty.

P p

Pussy cat, pussy cat, where have you been?
Under the waves in a submarine,
Pussy cat, pussy cat, what did you see?
A wobbly jellyfish goggling at me.

Q q

The Queen of Hearts she made some tarts,

From spiders, dust and soil

And broken bricks

And stones and sticks

And squirts of engine oil.

Rr

Rain, rain, go away,
You're shrinking me, I fear,
Please won't you stop?
Another drop
Will make me disappear.

S s

Simple Simon bought a pie,
But when he took a bite
A caterpillar wriggled out
To spoil his appetite.

T t

Twinkle, twinkle, little frog,
Shivering in your puddle,
Hop out of the soggy bog –
Come and have a cuddle.

U u

Up and down the city road,
Round and round the market,
Riding on my dinosaur,
Wherever can I park it?

V v

Vicky Sweet
Got both her feet
Stuck inside one shoe,
Now she bounces everywhere
Like a kangaroo.

W w

Wee Willie Winkie runs through the street,
Shoes on his hands, gloves on his feet,
People are pointing all over town,
Wee Willie Winkie's upside down.

Xx

X was an eXplorer,
He explored the mountain heights
In an orange balaclava
And a pair of purple tights.

Yy

Yankee Doodle came to town,
Did he take the bus?
No, he put a saddle
On a hippopotamus.

Z z

Zackary Dapp
Started to flap,
Started to flutter and squawk,
Climbed on a chair,
Jumped in the air
And flew round the room like a hawk.

Traditional Nursery Rhymes

Do you know any nursery rhymes that begin with A, V, X, or Z? No?
Well neither do we!

B

Bobby Shafto's gone to sea,
Silver buckles at his knee;
He'll come back and marry me,
Bonny Bobby Shafto!

C

Cock a doodle doo!
My dame has lost her shoe,
My master's lost his fiddlestick,
And knows not what to do.

D

Doctor Foster went to Gloucester
In a shower of rain;
He stepped in a puddle,
Right up to his middle,
And never went there again.

E

Elsie Marley is grown so fine,
She won't get up to feed the swine,
But lies in bed till eight or nine.
Lazy Elsie Marley.

F

Fee fi fo fum
I smell the blood of an Englishman.

G

Georgie Porgie, pudding and pie,
Kissed the girls and made them cry;
When the boys came out to play,
Georgie Porgie ran away.

H

Humpty Dumpty sat on a wall,
Humpty Dumpty had a great fall.
All the king's horses,
And all the king's men,
Couldn't put Humpty together again.

I

I had a little nut tree,
Nothing would it bear
But a silver nutmeg
And a golden pear.

J

Jack Sprat could eat no fat,
His wife could eat no lean,
And so between them both, you see,
They licked the platter clean.

K

Katie Beardie had a coo,
Black and white about the mou';
Wasna that a dentie coo?
Dance Katie Beardie!

L

Little Bo-Peep has lost her sheep,
And doesn't know where to find them;
Leave them alone, and they'll come home,
Bringing their tails behind them.

M

Mary, Mary, quite contrary,
How does your garden grow?
With silver bells and cockle shells,
And pretty maids all in a row.

N

Nellie Bligh
Caught a fly,
Tied it to a string;
String broke
Cut its throat,
Poor little thing.

O

Old King Cole
Was a merry old soul,
And a merry old soul was he;
He called for his pipe,
And he called for his bowl,
And he called for his fiddlers three.

P

Pussy cat, pussy cat, where have you
   been?
I've been to London to look at the
   queen.
Pussy cat, pussy cat, what did you
   there?
I frightened a little mouse under her
   chair.

Q

The Queen of Hearts
She made some tarts,
All on a summer's day;
The Knave of Hearts
He stole the tarts,
And took them clean away.

R

Rain, rain, go away,
Come again another day.

S

Simple Simon met a pieman,
Going to the fair;
Says Simple Simon to the pieman,
Let me taste your ware.

T

Twinkle, twinkle, little star,
How I wonder what you are!
Up above the world so high,
Like a diamond in the sky.

U

Up and down the City Road,
In and out the Eagle,
That's the way the money goes,
Pop goes the weasel!

W

Wee Willie Winkie runs through the
   town,
Upstairs and downstairs in his night
   gown,
Rapping at the window, crying through
   the lock,
Are the children all in bed, for now it's
   eight o'clock?

Y

Yankee Doodle came to town,
Riding on a pony;
He stuck a feather in his cap
And called it macaroni.